"A fearless discussion of an emotional issue with no-nonsense suggestions for parents concerned about the safety of their teenage daughters."
> —Patty Neal Dorian, North Carolina Coalition Against Domestic Violence

---

"From her experience with battered women, Patricia Gaddis has seen the need to be proactive by teaching young women how to steer clear of unhealthy relationships. *Dangerous Dating* answers that need. Immensely practical, filled with true-to-life stories, this book offers a wealth of information about the cycles and set-ups for abuse—and most importantly the way to avoid it!"
> —June Hunt, Hope for the Heart Ministries

"*Dangerous Dating* is must reading for parents and teens alike. Domestic violence has now moved beyond the boundaries of the home into the dating arena. Teenagers can become trapped in the clutches of violence and not know how to reach out for help. This book will help parents everywhere be on the alert for danger signs of this almost unthinkable problem."
> —James R. Beck, Ph.D., clinical psychologist and chair of the department of counseling, Denver Seminary

DANGEROUS

Dating

Helping Young Women Break Out of Abusive Relationships

by
Patricia Riddle Gaddis

SHAW

Dangerous Dating
A SHAW BOOK
PUBLISHED BY WATERBROOK PRESS
2375 Telstar Drive, Suite 160
Colorado Springs, CO 80920
A division of Random House, Inc.

All Scripture quotations, unless otherwise indicated, are taken from the HOLY BIBLE,
NEW INTERNATIONAL VERSION®. NIV®. Copyright © 1973, 1978, 1984 International
Bible Society. Used by permission of Zondervan Publishing House. All rights reserved.

The "NIV" and "New International Version" trademarks are registered in the United
States Patent and Trademark Office by International Bible Society. Use of either
trademark requires permission of International Bible Society.

Scripture quotations marked KJV are from the King James Version of the Bible.

Scripture quotations marked RSV are from the Revised Standard Version of the Bible,
copyright 1946, 1952, 1971 by the Division of Christian Education of the National
Council of the Churches of Christ in the USA, and used by permission.

The violence and nonviolence wheels on pages 50–51 are used by permission of the
Domestic Abuse Intervention Project, 202 East Superior St., Duluth, MN 55802; 218/
722-2781.

ISBN 0-87788-713-6

Copyright © 2000 by Patricia Riddle Gaddis

Cover design by Tobias Design
Interior design and typesetting by Carol Barnstable / Carol Graphics

Library of Congress Cataloging-in-Publication Data
Gaddis, Patricia Riddle.
    Dangerous dating : helping young women say no to abusive
    relationships / Patricia Gaddis.
        p.   cm.
    Includes bibliographical references.
    ISBN 0-87788-713-6 (pbk)
    1. Dating violence.   I. Title
HQ801.83.G34 2000
362.88—dc21   99-054941

03 02 01
6 5 4 3 2

To my goddaughters,
Rebecca and Emily;

And to my son,
Shawn—a real
champion for women.

Contents

Foreword 9

Introduction 13

1 Anna's Story 17

2 The Roots of Teen Dating Abuse 29

3 The Characteristics of Dating Abuse 45

4 Rescuing the Battered Teen 61

5 Prevention: Raising Assertive
  Daughters and Sons 81

6 When Your Daughter Marries
  Her Abuser 95

7 Getting Help 109

Appendix A: Are You Dating an Abusive
Male? Questions for Girls 117

Appendix B: Domestic Violence Resources
for Families 121

Appendix C: National Domestic Violence
Hotline/Resource Numbers (U.S.) 129

Appendix D: Miscellaneous Resources
for Parents and Teens 131

Notes 135

Foreword

As a father of two daughters who are about to enter their turbulent teen years, it sometimes frightens me when I consider the social climate in which they will have their initial dating encounters. Their mother and I have tried our best to instill within them a strong, biblically based concept of morality, and we will continue to do so as they travel through these years. I have confidence that my daughters possess a basic understanding of right and wrong, good and bad behavior.

But I am also a realist. I know that many of their young friends are already exploring their sexuality. I also know that not everybody with whom my daughters deal on a daily basis has the same value system. On the contrary, those attributes are now considered unusual by many teens and young adults.

Perhaps most disconcerting of all, I know that many of the young men my daughters will encounter will not play fair. Some will be users, others will be abusers, and some will attempt to heal their own wounds by inflicting hurt on my daughters.

How can I protect my daughters? What do I

need to know? Where can I go for help if I need it? These are a few of the crucial questions that Patricia Gaddis answers in *Dangerous Dating*, and as a dad, I am extremely grateful for her insights.

Her book is like a ray of light in a dark world. It sheds light on a subject that most of us would like to pretend did not exist—abusive dating relationships. Did you ever look at a young couple, shake your head, and say, "What does she see in that guy?" What she sees, of course, and what you see may be distinctly different. Worse yet, he may be an abuser who has an emotional hold stronger than a vise grip on that young woman. That hold can be broken, and Gaddis explains how it can be done effectively and safely. She does not hold back on this delicate subject. She writes with firmness, practical applications, and most of all, a compassion rarely found nowadays.

I must warn you, however, that what you are about to read is explosive. It may jolt you out of your cozy, comfortable world into a reality that you'd rather not know about—but if you are a parent of a teenager, or if you are a teen looking for some honest answers, this book could well be a lifesaver. When you are through reading, you will not wring your hands in despair, but you will breathe a sigh of relief and say, "Finally, someone has dared to tell me truth."

Ken Abraham
Author, *Don't Bite the Apple till You Check for Worms*

Introduction

Date rape. Rohypnol.* Abuse. Murder. It's a scary world out there. Sometimes I wonder how parents can even let their children leave the house. "Don't talk to strangers" is not enough anymore. More and more, children and teenagers are being hurt by people they know and trust. But how prevalent is dating abuse? After all, kids do fight. Teenagers' lives constantly erupt with drama and angst. Surely the stories we hear on the news about violent teens are exceptions. It can't really happen in my town, to my child. Can it? As a domestic violence counselor and advocate, I have facilitated numerous parenting classes, support groups, and life-skills programs for young, battered teens. Their stories of abuse are as extreme and humiliating as any that I have heard from adult victims. Let's put to rest these myths about dating violence. The following information is from *What Parents Need to Know about Dating Violence* by Barrie Levy and Patricia Occhiuzzo Giggans.[1]

*The date rape drug.

Misconception: "Abuse in teen relationships is not that common or serious."

Reality: Surveys show that at least 28 percent of teen relationships involve violence. According to the FBI, 20 percent of homicide victims are between the ages of fifteen and twenty-four, and one out of three women murdered in the U.S. is killed by a husband or boyfriend.

Misconception: "Guys who yell and hit just have bad tempers."

Reality: Abusers use violence to try to control another person. Abuse is made up of a series of behaviors, such as intimidation, threats, and isolation, as well as physical harm. Battering is not about anger so much as it is about power and control.

Misconception: "A guy has the right to discipline his girlfriend and show her who's boss."

Reality: Discipline is used to exercise authority, such as a parent has over a child or a superior over subordinates. Unfortunately, many societies have taught and encouraged men to dominate women under the guise of discipline.

Misconception: "Alcohol and/or drugs are what cause people to become violent and abusive."

Reality: Chemical substances are not the cause

of violence but may act as enablers to violence by lowering inhibitions.

Misconception: "Violence only happens between people who are poor or members of a minority."

Reality: Abuse in relationships exists among all classes, races, and cultural groups in society. It even happens in same-gender relationships.

Misconception: "Men who batter their wives or girlfriends are sociopaths."

Reality: Batterers are "normal" people that we encounter in everyday life. They can be the smartest, quietest, coolest young men or the best athletes on campus. What they all have in common is their inability to control their anger and aggressive impulses.

If you are a parent, you may have picked up this book because of a burning suspicion that your daughter is being abused by her boyfriend. Or perhaps you saw a movie or a television program on the topic of dating violence and found the subject to be a little too close to home. It is my hope that everyone who decides to read this book will gain a greater knowledge of dating violence and how it affects teens in our society.

In this book, I refer to abusers as *he* and victims as *she*. According to the U.S. Department of Justice, females experience ten times more domestic and dating abuse than do males. Even so, there are young women who abuse their boyfriends. I am not denying that here.

While the stories in these pages are true, the names and identifying details have been changed in order to ensure confidentiality.

Although this book is primarily for parents who wish to gather information on the topic of abuse, counselors and clergy may also gain a clearer understanding of the cycle of abuse that can occur between dating teenagers. If you are a battered teen and happen to find your story in the pages of my book, know that you are not alone! If you were given this book by a friend or family member, then someone cares about your dilemma and has taken the time to try to help you.

While I do not claim to offer a magical solution to the problem, it is my goal to share information that may be helpful, as well as guidelines and resources that will expand your range of vision on the dynamics of dating violence.

1 *Anna's Story*

The shrill ringing cut through my dreams, invading my sense of warmth and well-being. In a daze, I pressed the snooze button on my digital alarm, but to my dismay the annoying sound continued. Partially coherent, I reached for the telephone and whispered, "Hello."

"Good evening," responded the serene voice of my answering-service operator. "You have a domestic violence emergency at the hospital. Shall I inform the charge nurse that you'll call?"

Still in a half-dream state, I switched on the bedside lamp and shielded my eyes from the brightness. I instructed the telephone attendant to inform the hospital that I would be there as quickly as possible.

It was shortly after midnight, and I knew that most emergency room calls were very serious. As I reluctantly left the warmth of my bed, I resigned myself to the fact that I would probably not return home before dawn.

Although I had been a domestic violence counselor for many years, receiving a late-night call still disturbed me. I hurriedly combed my hair and brushed my teeth, wondering who was waiting for me at the hospital and just how badly she had been beaten. Moreover, would her abuser be lurking in the dark hospital parking lot—or pacing the hospital waiting room, making sure that everyone knew that he was in charge?

> *I wondered who was waiting for me at the hospital and how badly she had been beaten.*

I approached the hospital entrance and drove directly to the parking section labeled *EMERGENCY ROOM VISITORS ONLY.* I turned off the ignition and momentarily leaned back in my seat to collect my thoughts and check out my surroundings. Over the years I had received occasional threats from abusers, mainly because they had discovered that I had assisted their wives or girlfriends. This intimidation had caused me to become a little more cautious than the average person. There were only two other cars parked in the visitors' section, and both were unoccupied. I stepped out of my car and began walking toward the hospital entrance, staying in the well-lighted area. Before going inside, I paused to take in the Blue Ridge Mountain peaks that rose against the dark velvet sky and jeweled stars. *What a sight,* I thought, while breathing in the brisk winter air.

I announced my presence to the receptionist, and a nurse led me to a cubicle where my client, whom I will call Anna, was waiting. Like so many battered women that I have seen over the years, Anna looked as though she'd been in a terrible car crash. Unlike many of my clients, however, this broken, china-doll face belonged to a terrified teenager. Her long blond hair was caked with blood, and the entire right side of her face and neck was packed in gauze. An IV tube snaked along the bed railing and into her small, bruised hand. Slowly and painfully, Anna told her story.

Anna, who had recently turned eighteen, and her much older boyfriend, James, had been living together for six months. She had left her parents' home after a heated argument with her father regarding the college that he wanted her to attend.

Within just a few days, James began controlling Anna's every move. He slapped her around and constantly accused her of seeing other men while he was at work. He would not allow her to attend school or to contact her parents. Anna said that James had even threatened to kill her mother and father if she attempted to leave him.

Matters came to a head when Anna told James that she was pregnant. James beat her brutally. Then he held Anna at knifepoint for several hours and tried to force her to confess that the child she was carrying did not belong to him. Anna refused to acknowledge his accusation. After several hours of terrorizing her, James slashed her face and left their apartment in a rage, promising to finish her off when he returned. Anna managed to crawl into the bedroom and dial 911 for help.

"Did your parents know where you were staying all this time?" I asked.

"No," Anna replied weakly. "I just told them I was staying at a friend's house. I was afraid that James would kill them if they came around. Daddy pastors a church, and my mother might have a nervous breakdown if she knew the whole story."

"So you don't intend to tell your parents?" I asked.

"I wasn't going to, but somehow the police found out their names. I never meant for any of this to happen," Anna whispered. Her shock was beginning to wear off, and in its place came the horrible memories. "Now James will probably kill us all!"

"Don't worry," I said, touching her arm gently. "The charge nurse informed me that James has been arrested. Is going home with your parents an option? Will they be supportive?"

"I think so. But you won't tell them about the baby, will you?" she asked, in a small, scared voice. "They don't know about James. I met him at a party and never introduced him to my parents because he was older and I didn't think they'd approve."

"Everything you tell me is confidential," I promised.

"Just tell them I'm sorry," she said, "and that I love them very much. I didn't mean for this to happen!"

"It's not your fault," I told Anna quietly but firmly. "You didn't cause this to happen. James's actions were entirely his own. Nothing you said or did made him violent. You are the victim."

The nurses had advised me that Anna would be in surgery for a couple of hours, so I decided to stick around. Anna's parents appeared as I lifted a cup of strong black coffee from the beverage machine. Anna's father, a distinguished-looking man with dark hair, approached me just as I sat down in a cor-

> ## *Anna would be in surgery for a couple of hours*

ner of the waiting room. He extended his hand and introduced himself and his wife. His eyes were red-rimmed and full of pain. Anna's mother gazed numbly at the floor.

"One of the nurses told us that you are a counselor with the domestic violence shelter," Anna's father said. "My wife and I would like to know what we can do to get our daughter back. Can you help us?"

"I'm not a family therapist," I said, feeling drained and in need of collecting my thoughts. "My specialty is crisis intervention for victims of domestic violence."

"But can't you help us somehow?" he continued, his voice breaking. "I really don't know how much longer we can go on like this."

I suggested they take a seat while I went back

over to the snack machine for two more cups of coffee. I glanced at the large round clock on the wall above the door and then checked my watch. It was almost three o'clock in the morning, and I knew that my night was not nearing an end. Nevertheless, I felt tremendous sympathy for Anna's parents and knew that they needed support.

Lately I had noticed a significant rise at the clinic in cases involving young women and teens. I knew that many women in abusive relationships had grown up in abusive homes. But now I had begun seeing just as many teenage girls who came from stable environments. *Is Anna's father an abuser?* I wondered, as I pressed the appropriate selection for extra cream in his coffee. I glanced over my shoulder and noticed that the couple had joined hands and were quietly praying. Anna's father had placed a protective arm around his wife's shoulder. I felt comforted by their apparent alliance and concern for all that was going on in their daughter's life.

Anna's father rose courteously as I returned with the coffee. "I apologize for this inconvenience," he said. "It's just that my wife and I are at a total loss. Our daughter left home a little over six months ago, and although she has called us from time to time, she never revealed where she was staying. The guidance counselor informed us she had dropped out of school. That's just not like her. This is her last year, and she's always been a good student. We went to the police for help, but they told us there was nothing they could do because she is legally of age." He rubbed his eyes wearily and drew a ragged breath. "Then tonight we were awakened by two police officers at our door, telling us that Anna had been injured in a domestic dispute with her boyfriend. We didn't know that Anna had a boyfriend! I've dealt with a few domestic violence cases in the church that I pastor, but never would I have dreamed that our own daughter could become mixed up in something like this!"

Anna's mother spoke for the first time. "Anna worked so hard at school, she never really had time for boys," she said flatly, her eyes still on the floor. "But things changed over the summer. Anna got a job and started spending more time going out with friends. She had a list of books to read and research to do to get ready for her senior honors classes, but she wasn't working on it. We had a lot of arguments."

Anna's mother took a sip of coffee and then continued. "The big one started when Anna and John got into an argument over which college she

should attend. It was a silly quarrel, and I've been ir-
ritated with John since the day it happened. What
difference does it make if Anna doesn't attend your
alma mater?" she said, finally lifting her head. Her
eyes blazed with hurt so bright that her husband
momentarily looked away.

"I'll admit that I expected a lot from Anna—
maybe more than she was able to give," he said finally. His voice thickened with emotion. "But I sure
didn't see this tragedy knocking on our door!"

We sat in silence for a full minute. Finally Anna's
mother spoke. "Neither of us had spent a lot of time
with Anna in the weeks before she left," she mur-
mured, her delicate features softening as she took her
husband's hand. "In retrospect, I realize that something was very wrong in our daughter's life. But I
never dreamed it could be something like this!"

> ### *All of the warning signs had been there.*

As we further discussed Anna's situation, I realized that all of the warning signs had been there. In
one instance, Anna's mother had noticed a large

bruise on her daughter's arm. When she asked what had happened, Anna told her mother that she had fallen in gym class. A short time later, when Anna came home with a swollen lip, she again said that she had tripped while playing basketball. While her mother was somewhat skeptical about this explanation, she had no reason to believe her daughter would lie. Trust is, after all, the most sacred bond that we can ever hope to have with those we dearly love. Yet all of the late nights and weekends when Anna told her parents that she was with friends, she was really spending time with James.

Soon the situation was out of hand, and Anna was caught between her boyfriend's demands and her parents' trust. Her grades rapidly dropped, and she seemed depressed. Her father became worried that she might not make it into the college that he wanted her to attend. Moreover, he was convinced that she would not make it into any college at all unless she did a quick turnaround. Angrily confronting Anna, he demanded that she study harder and stop spending so many weekends with her friends.

"Either stay home and hit the books," he said, "or prepare to flip hamburgers for the rest of your life!"

Anna felt like a total failure. James was demanding more and more of her time. If she suddenly stopped seeing him on weekends, he would be furious! But how could she tell her parents about this secret relationship? They had trusted her. If they knew about her weekend escapades, they would never let her out of their sight again!

Anna described James's behavior then as sometimes loving while at other times quite cruel. "He was like two different people," she said. "One small disagreement would lead to another, and the next thing I knew he was slamming me against the wall or twisting my arm. Then, after a day or so, his anger would wear off and we'd make up. He'd tell me how sorry he was for accusing me of looking at other guys. I thought he was jealous because he loved me so much."

Anna's nightmare might have been resolved with an open dialogue with her parents. But Anna's parents felt trapped by their own trust, believing their daughter would misunderstand them if they questioned her activities. Unfortunately, Anna was simply not ready for the total independence that had accompanied her parents' naïve faith in her. Trust without accountability can often prove disastrous.

I am pleased to report that Anna's story has a

happy ending. She returned home to her parents and six months later gave birth to a baby girl. Shortly after James was released from jail, he began to harass Anna and her parents. He backed off, however, when her father hired an attorney and threatened to take legal action. Anna finished high school and eventually completed a degree in nursing. Her life as a young single mother has not been easy, but she credits her success to her parents who loved her unconditionally.

2 *The Roots of Teen Dating Abuse*

What makes some teens more likely than others to be involved in dating violence? Is abuse a phenomenon of only certain economic levels, geographical areas, cultures, or family structures? Donna Shalala, Secretary of the U.S. Department of Health and Human Services, said in a CNN interview, "In this country domestic violence is just about as common as giving birth." We have only to look back to 1995, to the case of Nicole Brown Simpson and her ex-husband, football star and actor O. J. Simpson, to see that domestic violence happens to the wealthy as well as the poor and to the majority group as well as minority groups. Clearly, the roots of abuse lie far deeper than demographics.

From the Beginning of Time

Throughout the ages, violence against women has been upheld by both civil and religious authorities.[2] Anthropologists have discovered Egyptian papyrus documents from as early as 2000 B.C. that describe sexual violence against women. X rays of female mummies show six to eight times more skull fractures and breaks than do X rays of male mummies.

During medieval times, women lost the ground that had been gained through the spiritual teachings of Jesus. Eve's transgression was used as a justification for keeping all women in a subordinate social position: "The woman whom thou gavest to be with me, she gave me of the tree, and I did eat" (Genesis 3:12, KJV). Consequently, violence against women has been an acceptable practice in Western culture since the early Middle Ages. The history of our language reveals fascinating legal perspectives on abuse. For example, the source of the common

English law allowed a man to beat his wife so long as the switch was no thicker than his thumb.

expression "rule of thumb" originates from English common law, making it permissible for a man to beat his wife, so long as he did so with a switch no thicker than his thumb![3]

Nineteenth-century feminists believed that male tyranny would totally disappear when women gained the right to vote, own property, and have equal protection under the law. Little did they know that a century later, domestic violence would be the leading cause of death and injury to women between the ages of fifteen and forty-four. Until the late 1970s, domestic abuse, while against the law, was rarely prosecuted. The courts considered it a "family matter."

Charlotte's Story

Charlotte had been out of an abusive relationship for five years when she came to talk with me. Her sixteen-year-old daughter, Jeannie, was in the intensive care unit of the hospital because her boyfriend had beaten her so badly that she sustained severe internal injuries.

"I knew she was in trouble when he started calling her all the time, insisting that she keep him constantly informed of her whereabouts," Charlotte said. "But when I tried to tell Jeannie that she was headed for trouble, she just wouldn't listen. She became so mad at me for trying to interfere with her life that she moved in with her father. He allowed her to quit school and then bought her a car! Every time Jeannie and her dad had an argument, she would come back to my place. That didn't last long,

> *Young girls who come from abusive homes gravitate toward abusive relationships.*

though, because I asked her about the marks on her arms and neck. She knew how much I disliked her boyfriend, so we just couldn't get along. All the while, she insisted that he wasn't abusing her. But I knew better. I had lived with abuse for nearly ten years, and I don't know how she thought she could fool me!"

Charlotte had endured years of violence from her ex-husband before she had been through our program for legal advocacy and shelter. Unfortunately, many young girls who come from abusive homes seem to gravitate toward abusive relationships. Charlotte herself was the child of an abusive father. Her mother endured abuse all of her married life; divorce was never an option due to her religious convictions.

Charlotte's daughter, Jeannie, eventually recovered from her injuries, yet she continued to drift from one abusive relationship to another until at last she married someone who was very violent. Consequently, the torch of abuse was passed on through three generations.

All in the Family

While the roots of abuse lie deep in history, the family has provided much of the nourishment for dating violence, not only among battered teens but also among their abusers. Most psychologists agree that temper tantrums, acting out in school, and hitting other children, when gone unchecked, indicate a potential for adolescent and adult offenses. Abuse is also part of a vicious cycle that is passed on from one generation to the next. Very often boys are taught by their own fathers to be "in charge," especially in their relationships with women. When this attitude gets out of hand, it becomes abusive.[4]

Social scientists have a variety of techniques

with which to measure how power is distributed within the family.[5] The most widely used method is based on who makes the final decision on a number of crucial issues, such as who has the final say on buying a car, a house, or having children. Families unable to distribute power in the decision-making process have a greater chance of developing unhealthy and even violent patterns of behavior. Studies indicate that a more democratic family system poses less threat of violence. Unfortunately, nurturing a democratic family system is not a skill that can be learned by a child raised in an abusive environment.

Children who are brought up in violent homes seem to have an entirely different perspective on violence in our society. For example, a thirty-three-year-old convict, imprisoned for most of his adult life for violent assaults, told his psychiatrist: "Violence is, in a way, like bad language—something that a person like me has been brought up with, something I got used to early on as a part of the daily scene of childhood."[6]

Abuse often begets abuse, especially if the marriage continues until the children are older. By this time they have become entrenched in the violence and are poised to carry on the fury to the next generation. Children who are younger seem to have a greater chance of escaping the fury of future violent relationships because they have a larger window of time in which to heal before getting involved in their own relationships.

> *Teens with low self-esteem feel powerless to stand up for themselves in a harmful relationship.*

"I'm Not Worthy"

Young women prone to being abused often share a common bond of very low self-esteem. They may have seen their mothers abused and have assumed that women are not important enough to be treated with respect. They may have bought into media messages that women exist to please men, and they may have been denied affection, praise, and affirmation throughout childhood. Teens with low self-esteem feel powerless to stand up for themselves in a harmful relationship.

What happens to self-esteem? As children grow,

the differences between boys and girls become increasingly obvious. Girls are on average more physically mature than boys and are less susceptible to illness. They suffer less from speech, learning, and behavior disorders, mental retardation, and sleep disorders. As a group, girls speak and write earlier and more fluently. They tend to be more adept at grammar and spelling, yet less skilled at manipulating objects, constructing three-dimensional forms, and mentally manipulating figures and pictures. These are generalizations, of course, based on studies of large groups.[7] Certainly there is room for a vast amount of variation within individuals. But to what degree are these tendencies learned rather than genetic?

Max and Carol were careful to dress their baby daughter, Alicia, in blue jeans and give her trucks to play with. As Alicia grew, Carol and Max encouraged their daughter's interests—sports and science as well as books and music. Alicia knew that she could become anything—a doctor, a dancer, a builder, a firefighter, even president. But Max and Carol were ill prepared for what happened when their daughter reached adolescence. Alicia's grades fell. She dropped out of her after-school clubs and began spending more and more time in her room. She became erratic in her appearance, wearing a baggy, unwashed sweatshirt one day and a short, clingy dress the next.

In her bestseller, *Reviving Ophelia*, Mary Pipher describes vividly how the self-esteem of even the strongest girls can plummet with adolescence.[8] Suddenly their world no longer values intelligence, strength, imagination, and courage. Their world says, "Lose ten pounds fast"; "Wear these jeans and you'll be popular"; "Boys like girls who . . ." In adolescence, both boys and girls look less to their parents and more to their peers and their subculture to find their own identity. Our society encourages boys to achieve, compete, act independently, and assume personal responsibility. Girls, on the other hand, are encouraged to be reflective, beautiful, obedient, and submissive.

Over the years I have discovered that most members of my gender do not like themselves very much. Whether we are prized homemakers, highly paid business executives, or celebrities, we may be paralyzed by poor body image, economic disadvantages, and the loss of our true selves. We believe that we are too tall or too short or too fat. Advertisers sell us a look that we try to mimic, making many of us forever unable to appreciate our own uniqueness. A young girl who does not have a good sense of identity and who feels inadequate and unloved is a prime target for victimization.

Seven Going on Seventeen

In my work with thousands of teens via classrooms, support groups, and shelters, I have realized that the media, along with our own culture, encourages young girls to grow up long before their time. Proms that were once reserved for high school seniors are now in vogue for middle school students. Children in kindergarten have graduation ceremonies, complete with cap and gown. Of course, no one can argue with the fact that these children look adorable, but are we as a society forcing our children to grow up long before they are equipped for the obstacles that accompany adulthood?

Not long ago I saw a television documentary on beauty pageants for children.[9] I was stunned by the amount of competition between girls who were obviously too young to even know why they were competing. These children were dressed as miniature adults, wearing elaborate jewelry and heavy makeup. One mother of a six year old stated that she had frosted her daughter's dark blond hair in order to make it appear brighter beneath the lights. Another proud stage parent boasted that her seven year old could apply eyeliner and mascara better than a makeup artist. These little girls were being groomed for adult pageants, and one charming eight year old told reporters that she was planning to become Miss America in the year 2011!

All of the mothers claimed that beauty pageants bolstered their daughters' self-esteem. I wondered, however, how this display could do anything other than squash a playful childhood and suppress the development of an inner, spiritual loveliness that would carry these little girls beyond the world of outward appearances and through the "wrinkles" of life. When the children were asked what they liked most about beauty pageants, they stated that it gave them an opportunity to meet other children. Yet when questioned what they most disliked about pageants, all of the little girls agreed that they hated wearing mascara and getting their hair sprayed! Second on the list was the uncomfortable costumes. "But you just *love* doing this, don't you, sweetie?" crooned one mother. Her little daughter quickly responded by saying that she did love beauty pageants, and it really wasn't so bad.

Until the seventeenth century, parents dressed

their children as small adults and had little aware-ness of the special needs of children.[10] During America's colonial period, most people believed that children differed from adults only in size and experience. In Louisa May Alcott's famous novel, *Little Women*, the main character, Jo, was fre-quently frowned on for acting like a vivacious child

> *Integrating children into adulthood too soon can fracture the fragile boundaries of young girls.*

instead of a little lady. Young girls of that time were expected to act like "little women." As the years pro-gressed, scientific research helped us to understand that intelligence and maturity develop in stages ac-cording to age.

I believe that we make a dangerous mistake when we press our children to grow up too soon. Integrating children into adulthood too soon can fracture the fragile boundaries of young girls. How can we, as a society, dress our children to look and act like little adults and then expect them to have

the necessary skills with which to protect themselves? Is it suitable to dress a five-year-old girl as a
miniature sex symbol and then expect her to defend
herself as an adult when faced with sexual ad-
vances? Calvin Klein's preoccupation with the public sexualization of underage girls began in 1982
with the child-model Brooke Shields, who pro-
claimed that nothing could come between her and
her Calvins. A decade later, teen-model Kate Moss
began showing Klein's clothing line. She frequently
appeared in reputable women's magazines. Sometimes she was topless with arms crossed over her
breasts and wearing jeans. In other shots she sat
partially nude and in the lap of a male model. Moss
later appeared in *Playboy,* and though of legal age
when posing nude, her appeal, according to top
photographers and designers, was that she appeared to be about fourteen.[11]

New York Times columnist Elizabeth Kaye
wrote: "In a culture where images generally wield
more power than words, the public has become ac-
customed to the child-woman, . . . fragile and vul-
nerable to the point of breaking. Like a piece of
fruit, they are cheaper for being slightly damaged;
like all little girls, they seem easier to manipulate
than grown-up women."[12]

Love Hurts

Sexuality and violence have become increasingly bound up with each other in American society. Teenage girls experience one of the highest rates of violence by an intimate partner compared to other

> *Sexuality and violence are increasingly bound up with each other in American society.*

age groups.[13] While the focus of my book is on violence between dating teens, and not rape specifically, the fact remains that a significant percentage of both adult and teen victims of abuse are forced to have sexual intercourse during episodes of physical violence. This may account in part for the high frequency of teen pregnancies in America. According to the Centers for Disease Control, about one million teens become pregnant each year; 95 percent of those pregnancies are unintended, and almost one-third end in abortion. In an abusive relationship, one partner is in control of the other and maintains power by threats and derogatory comments. Often the abuser will force his girlfriend to participate in sexual acts against her will. It is not at all uncommon for abused teenage girls to become pregnant during an episode of violence that included forced intercourse.[14]

For most of us, I suspect, the sex education we received at school and at home was quite a bit different from what we learned in the hallways and on the playground. The films about egg and sperm did little to help us develop sexual values, come to terms with our own sexuality, and learn to make sexual choices. That has not changed much. Teens are still confused. Combine this confusion with the incredibly mixed messages coming from magazines, movies, sitcoms, and the evening news, and it is no wonder that so many girls are falling into harmful relationships. We see and hear about sex in connection with love, anger, marriage, sin, fun, rebellion, music, and fashion. Sex is used to sell everything from shampoo and cereal to cars and insurance.

Teens, both girls and boys, have a hard enough time coping with emerging sexuality. They are maturing physically much faster than they are emotionally and socially. When they see sex distorted into manipulation and violence, most teens do not have the maturity to filter out the wrong ideas and false values. Abusive relationships are by definition highly emotional. Both the abuser and the abused react from instinct—instincts formed under the influence of questionable and even harmful sources.

Many people believe that the only way to prevent domestic violence is to change the attitudes that foster abuse in our society. Studies reveal at least as high a prevalence of physical violence among dating couples as married couples.[15] Further research shows that more than 50 percent of all women will experience some form of violence from their intimate partners.[16] Some 30 percent of women murdered in the U.S. are murdered by their husbands, ex-husbands, or boyfriends.[17] Clearly, the greatest risk factor for being abused in a dating relationship is being born female, making it all the more crucial for parents to take extra care in helping their daughters to develop good self-esteem and healthy boundaries.

3 The Characteristics of Dating Abuse

Teen dating violence is often characterized by the same patterns of controlling behavior that occur in abusive adult relationships. However, the peer pressure and levels of vulnerability that characterize a teenager's stage of development make teen battering unique. Because young girls are inexperienced in relationships, they will find it far more difficult to manage the conflict, decisions, and emotions that arise. In addition, far fewer options are available for teenage girls who are seeking help. They have fewer opportunities for economic independence, and most domestic violence shelters are unable to accommodate teenage girls, mainly because of the legal liabilities that are involved when sheltering minors.

Battering is a complex problem with no simple solutions. Unfortunately, there is no exact blueprint that you can follow to ensure your daughter's safety. By the time teens begin experimenting with their own dating relationships, they have been bombarded with messages that violence against women is acceptable. Violence usually surfaces over a period of time, but the warning signals are there from the beginning.

The Stages of Abuse

Domestic violence professionals who have studied violence between intimates describe three phases of abuse. It is crucial for parents and counselors to be able to identify these phases and recognize the characteristics of both the battered teen and her abuser. In recognizing these patterns, we can begin to predict when violence may erupt. These are the cyclical stages of abuse:[18]

Phase one is a period of growing tension that is characterized by sudden changes in the abuser's temperament or mood. During this phase of the cycle, the abuser becomes more irritable and tends to

> *During the "honeymoon" phase the abuser will enthusiastically court his girlfriend.*

react negatively to frustration. The victim may become more nurturing and compliant towards her abuser, keeping her distance and not showing any anger toward him. Encouraged by her passive acceptance, the abuser will then become more argumentative and may accuse her of spending too much time with her family and not enough time with him. He may also insist that she is flirting with other boys.

Phase two involves an explosion of anger and violence that is characterized by physical assault. During this interval the abuser will harm his victim through various methods, including stalking, threatening her family, or sexually and physically abusing her.

Phase three is commonly referred to by domestic violence advocates as the "honeymoon" or "hearts and flowers" phase. During phase three the abuser will begin an enthusiastic courtship with his girlfriend, sending her flowers or romantic notes and telling her that he wants them to begin anew. He may tell her that he did not mean to hurt her; he may blame someone else for his offenses. Phase three may last for a few days or a few months, but in most cases it will eventually stop altogether. When this happens, the battered teen will find little respite from the abuse.

Let's take a look at each of the stages in more detail.

Phase One—the Lit Fuse

Anna recalled that in the early days of living together, she tried very hard not to do anything that would upset James or "set him off." While in this stage he would accuse her of dressing too provocatively or flirting with other boys. When Anna tried to forestall his impending explosion by giving him extra affection, he became even more intensely jealous and possessive, asking her if this was how she acted toward other guys when he was not around.

James insisted that Anna carry a cell phone so that he could get in touch with her at any time throughout the day. If she walked to the corner store for a snack and forgot to take her cell phone along, he would cross-examine her for hours, wanting to know exactly who she had seen at the store and how much money she had spent and demanding to see the cash register receipt. At the outset of their relationship, Anna felt flattered by her boyfriend's attention, mistaking jealousy for love. But as time progressed, she felt confused and frightened by his behavior.

Domestic violence counselors see a very strong connection between controlling attitudes and abuse. The violence and nonviolence wheels (next pages) are helpful graphics for assisting victims of dating and domestic abuse. Most domestic violence counselors use the violence and nonviolence wheels as an educational and assessment tool for women in abusive marriages. While teen victims and perpetrators may not be able to relate to some of the signs and symptoms as outlined on the wheels, the central theme of the violence wheel is *power and control,* and this is what dominates the abuser's behavior. If a girl is in an abusive dating relationship, she will recognize a number of the characteristics described in the violence wheel.[19]

A girl in a violent or controlling relationship will need to begin to think about what a healthy relationship will look like. The nonviolence wheel (page 51) describes such a relationship. The central

Using Privilege: Treating her like a servant; making all the big decisions; acting like the "master of the castle"; being the one to define roles

Using Children: Making her feel guilty about the children; threatening to take the children away; (if separated) using the children to relay messages; using visitation to harass her

Minimizing, Denying, and Blaming: Making light of the abuse and not taking her concerns about it seriously; saying the abuse didn't happen; shifting responsibility for abusive behavior; saying she caused it

Using Isolation: Controlling what she does, who she sees and talks to, what she reads, where she goes; limiting outside involvement; using jealousy to justify actions

Using Emotional Abuse: Putting her down; making her feel bad about herself; calling her names; making her think she's crazy; playing mind games; humiliating her; making her feel guilty

Using Intimidation: Making her afraid by using looks, actions, gestures; smashing things; destroying her property; abusing pets; displaying weapons

Using Coercion and Threats: Making and/or carrying out threats to do something to hurt her; threatening to leave her; threatening to commit suicide; threatening to report her to welfare or other government agency; making her drop legal charges; making her do illegal things

Using Economic Abuse: Preventing her from getting or keeping a job; making her ask for money; taking her money; not letting her know about or have access to family income

Shared Responsibility: Mutually agreeing on a fair distribution of work; making family decisions together

Responsible Parenting: Sharing parental responsibilities; being a positive, nonviolent role model for children

Honesty and Accountability: Accepting responsibility for self; acknowledging responsibility for past use of violence; admitting being wrong; communicating openly and truthfully

Trust and Support: Supporting her goals in life; respecting her right to her own feelings, friends, activities, and opinions

Respect: Listening to her nonjudgmentally; being emotionally affirming and understanding; valuing opinions

Nonthreatening Behavior: Talking and acting so that she feels safe and comfortable expressing herself and doing things

Negotiation and Fairness: Seeking mutually satisfying resolutions to conflicts; accepting change; being willing to compromise

Economic Partnership: Making money decisions together; making sure both partners benefit from financial arrangements

theme of the nonviolence wheel is *equality,* and this graphic reflects the functional system of partnership and shared responsibility.[20]

Phase two—the Explosion

It was during phase two of the cycle that Anna was seriously harmed and could have died from her boyfriend's assault. Unfortunately, she had to endure many cycles through this dangerous phase before finally getting out of the violence. Finding a safe place for your daughter during this critical phase could save her life, but in Anna's case, her parents did not know where she was and could not intervene.

Although the most obvious signs of phase two are physical injuries, emotional and psychological abuses are just as prevalent and, in many ways, just as harmful. It is not unusual for the abuser to threaten harm against his victim's family or friends. He may say things such as: "If I can't have you, then no one else can" or "Your parents will pay for the way that you treat me."

Anna lived under the constant fear that James would kill her and her parents if she left him. She stated to me that she would have left him a short time after having moved in with him if he had not threatened to kill her mother and father.

"He would say over and over again that he would kill me, my mom, and my dad if I ever left him," Anna said. "I relived his threats again and again whenever I thought about escaping. I couldn't bear the thought of placing my parents in that kind of situation."

With psychological abuse, the abuser may also force his girlfriend to leave her family and friends, quit her job, and become financially dependent on him. He may control where she goes and how long she stays.

> *In both adult and teen cases, fear often keeps the victim from leaving her abuser.*

After Anna moved in with her boyfriend, James would not allow her to contact her parents, and so her calls to them were made in secret. "They would ask me where I was staying and if I was ever going to come home," Anna said. "I would tell them not to worry—that I was staying with friends. I just could not place them at risk! It was horrible."

In both adult and teen cases of dating violence, fear often keeps the victim from leaving her abuser. According to the National Coalition against Domestic Violence, a woman's chances of being murdered by her abusive partner rise by 75 percent when she leaves him.

Phase Three—Promises

Anna clearly remembered the "honeymoon" stage of their relationship. During phase three she readily forgave James for his threats and harassing phone calls, and his princely manner filled her with hope. James routinely blamed others for his anger: his boss for harassing him, his job for making him tense, and other men for making him jealous and suspicious.

In phase three, the romance in the relationship returns, and the victim may believe that her boyfriend will never try to hurt her again. She may become angry at her friends or parents for reminding her of the stalking, the phone calls, and her visits to the emergency room that were due to her boyfriend's violence.

In Anna's situation, the honeymoon phases became shorter and less frequent. Eventually, the cy cle began to go back and forth between phases one and two with no intervening phase three. When this happened, the physical assaults become more frequent. Anna recalled feeling as though she were trapped in a perpetual nightmare. "I didn't know about the three phases of abuse then," Anna said. "I was just so confused by James's erratic behavior! After a while, there were no more honeymoon phases. I kept wondering when James would return to his good side again. He never did."

Reading the Signs

There are typical signs and behaviors that are likely to develop if a teen is becoming involved in a potentially harmful relationship. Recognizing these signs is the first step toward removing your daughter from danger before she is seriously injured.

The Potential Victim

Your daughter may not openly say anything about the relationship and her confusion and fear. Her behavior, however, may give some clues. Watch for these signs:

❖ Has your daughter given up things that were once very important to her?

❖ Has she become distant from her friends? Have her long-term goals changed?

❖ At times does your daughter seem afraid of her boyfriend?

❖ Is she startled when the phone rings?

❖ Is she evasive about their plans and dating activities?

❖ Have you overheard her explaining to her boyfriend why she was late getting home, along with all of the details of her day?

❖ Does he make most or all of the decisions about what they will do, where they will go, with whom they will socialize?

❖ Does he frequently call and want to know where she is?

❖ Does she make excuses for his jealous behavior? ("He loves me so much that he doesn't want us to be apart." "I acted badly, and he just lost his temper.")

❖ Have you observed him losing his temper toward your daughter or someone else?

❖ Have her grooming habits declined since becoming involved with him? His possessiveness may be preventing her from taking the extra time that she once spent on her personal appearance. She may also be fearful of attracting another boy's attention.

❖ Has she suddenly lost weight? The obsession with body image, along with the very narrow definition of attractiveness in our society, can be particularly cruel tools that the abusive male may use to control his girlfriend.

❖ Does your daughter have unexplained injuries (bruises on her neck, an unexplained limp, a cut lip, for example)?

❖ Does she seem depressed? Does she refrain from conversation? Does she seem to operate in a world where no one else may enter? Are her comments about life negative?

✤ Does she apologize for everything and criticize herself? Her already shaky self-esteem will plummet even further as she becomes more deeply involved in the relationship.

The Potential Abuser

A potential abuser's behavior will be filled with inconsistencies. He will naturally try to make himself look good to friends and relatives. His need for power and his uncontrollable temper, however, will eventually give him away. Here are some characteristics of an abuser:

✤ He has a negative attitude toward women. ("Girls are just not as smart as boys!" "Women need to stay in their place!")

✤ He seems "bossy"; he makes decisions without consulting others.

✤ He exhibits mood swings.

✤ He is excessively jealous and possessive. He may question his girlfriend extensively about what she is doing outside of his presence. Or he may try the other extreme, pretending weakness and neediness to keep her focused on him.

✤ He may prevent his girlfriend from seeing her family and friends.

✤ He may admit to having witnessed his father abusing his mother. All studies indicate that battering is learned behavior. Males who have a family history of observing or experiencing abuse are more likely to be abusive, violent, and sexually aggressive.[21]

✤ He lacks the ability to trust his girlfriend and cannot appropriately express anger without becoming violent.

✤ He blames the victim for his violent behavior. ("If you hadn't been flirting with other guys, I wouldn't have lost my temper.")

✤ He denies that he has abused his girlfriend, despite bruises and other evidence. ("I just gave her a little playful push and she fell because she wasn't paying attention!")

A common complaint among parents of teens is that they suddenly feel shut out of their children's lives. Anna removed herself physically from her home, and her parents had no idea what was happening to her or that she needed help. A battered teen who is too confused and frightened to save herself, or to reach out to those who love her, has little hope of escaping her nightmare. For this reason, it is crucial for parents, educators, and clergy to become more aware of teen dating violence so young girls at risk may receive the help they need.

4 Rescuing the Battered Teen

Thirty-one-year-old Gail will probably reside in a skilled nursing facility for the rest of her life. Thirteen years ago, her boyfriend angrily pushed her out of his car on a busy interstate highway, and she was hit by an oncoming car. Now a paraplegic, she must receive twenty-four-hour medical care. Gail's abusive boyfriend was given a four-year prison sentence plus three years' supervised probation for his crime. Gail, on the other hand, will remain forever imprisoned within her injured body. She sits helplessly in a wheelchair, staring vacantly out her window, sometimes spilling tears of frustration when old friends visit and she cannot remember their names.

Eighteen-year-old Amy was another tragedy of

dating violence. When we first met, she was in the hospital recovering from a severe beating. Her boyfriend was an intravenous drug user, and during their time together she contracted HIV. Two years after my first encounter with her, Amy died of AIDS. Not all stories of abuse have unhappy endings, but many teenage girls die at the hands of their abusers. Other casualties of dating violence sustain injuries so severe that they never fully recover. If you suspect that your daughter's boyfriend is abusing her, I urge you to intervene now.

Sarah's Story

My good friend, Susan, never allows her teenage girls to attend a party without checking out their plans in advance. By following this strategy, she actually saved her fifteen-year-old daughter, Sarah, from becoming deeply involved in a violent relationship.

Susan's approach was simple. When one of her girls asked permission to attend a party at the home of a friend, she picked up the phone and checked things out without being obvious about it. She did this by asking the parents of the friend if they needed additional refreshments for the party and verifying the chaperone arrangements. Her rationale for snooping is her belief that teens have a far more elaborate network of support than adults, making it difficult for parents to keep up with their kids' activities. She believes that kids cover for each other while parents are left standing on the sidelines, wondering what is going on. During one of her routine investigations there came the dreaded response from the parent: "What party are you talk-

> **Susan was crushed to have discovered that Sarah had lied to her.**

ing about?" Susan hurriedly apologized, explaining that she must have misunderstood her daughter. She was crushed to have discovered that Sarah had lied to her about a nonexistent party. She wondered if Sarah's boyfriend, Tom, had anything to do with it.

Susan had no reason to believe that her daughter's relationship with Tom was unhealthy. She had, however, expressed concern about their age difference. Tom was a senior and Sarah only a freshman.

When my friend sat down with her daughter to discuss the fabricated story, Sarah blurted out the truth. She was afraid of Tom but did not know how to break it off with him. At first, they had been nothing more than friends. Then they began dating, and Tom pushed her to become sexually involved. When Sarah refused, he became violent and threatened to cause problems for her entire family if she stopped seeing him. He even began spreading false accusations around the school that her father, a family-care physician, was performing abortions. This really frightened Sarah because she did not want her father's reputation destroyed. The more compelled Sarah felt to protect her family, the more she put up with Tom's abusive treatment. The more she put up with, the more ashamed she became, making it more difficult for her to tell anyone what was really going on.

Susan was stunned. Sarah pulled up her long sleeves to reveal numerous bruises on her arms. Susan recalled seeing several bruises on her daughter over the past few weeks. Guilt shot through her as she realized she hadn't even asked Sarah where the bruises had come from.

"My husband and I prayed about the matter and decided that we wanted Sarah as far away from Tom as possible," Susan said.

So Sarah's parents removed her from the local high school and placed her in a private boarding school for girls. At first, Sarah did not like the idea of having to leave her classmates behind. Susan believed, however, that the negative peer pressure from Sarah's friends had contributed to the problem.

"When Sarah first entered high school," recalled Susan, "she wanted to try out for cheerleading. I felt uneasy about this, mainly because I didn't want her to become involved with the 'popular' crowd at school. I wanted to protect her from all of the peer pressure. But we eventually gave in to her wishes. Soon after that I began to notice a change in Sarah's attitude—nothing major, but I thought she seemed a bit more arrogant toward her younger sisters. She talked a lot about the importance of being popular in school. I found myself correcting her when she made negative comments about students in her class who did not have steady boyfriends. Sarah told us later that her friends had put enormous pressure on her to stay involved with Tom because he was the most popular boy in school!"

Sarah adjusted well to boarding school and joined the student government. She also attends counseling sessions on a regular basis and, according to her mother, has gained a better understanding of the peer pressure that propelled her toward an unhealthy relationship.

"Because of Sarah's bad experience, our younger daughters are more alert to the dangers involved in abusive relationships," Susan said. "While I don't regret checking out my children's party plans, I have made communication with my teens a top priority. I've learned that spending time with them and talking to them, even if they don't want to talk to me, is very important. Now, if one of my daughters has the smallest bruise on her arm or leg, I specifically ask her about it. It never even occurred to me that my own child could be involved in a violent relationship! I am so very grateful to God that her father and I became aware of the situation in time to do something about it."

Studies consistently reveal that most teens in abusive relationships have not talked with any adults about the violence in their lives.[22] Consequently, it is crucial that parents with teens learn to identify the barriers to communication and encourage dialogue on the topic.

Susan's technique of checking out her children's party plans may seem a bit underhanded. Many would argue that she should have trusted her teenage daughter, never questioning her plans or party arrangements beyond a curfew. Yet remember Anna. Her parents trusted her unconditionally, and in doing so, placed her in a situation so awkward that she felt unable to tell them the truth.

Perhaps both families erred, Anna's in trusting too much and Susan's in being overly cautious. Yet given the fact that 20 percent of all homicide victims are between the ages of fifteen and twenty-four, it seems wise for parents to err on the side of caution.

Taking the First Steps

If you suspect your daughter is being abused or is in a potentially dangerous relationship, the first thing to do is to be sure of the facts. Study the three phases of abuse and the characteristics of the battered teen that are discussed in chapter 3. Which ones, if any, ring true for your daughter?

Then talk with your daughter and tell her your concerns. Assure her that you are on her side. She may, like Sarah, welcome the chance to unload her burden. Or, she may deny there is a problem and assure you that everything is fine. Or, she may resent your interference and think only that you are trying to break up the relationship. Whatever her response, don't give up. If she rejects you, you may need to seek outside help.

> *In my experience, a non-judgmental but candid approach to the issue yields results.*

When working with teens, I never fail to tell them that violent relationships can be deadly. I tell them about clients of mine, like Gail and Amy, who did not escape their abusers. I quote statistics with great candor while discussing not only the danger to their lives, but also the risks of HIV and unwanted pregnancy. I have found that teenagers are actually more receptive to these statistics and risk factors than adult victims of abuse. Many of these girls unfortunately go back to their abusive boyfriends several times before making the final break. In my experience, however, a nonjudgmental but candid approach to the issue yields results. If you have discovered that your teen is involved in an abusive dating relationship, I urge you to be frank with her. If she doesn't believe you, find someone she might believe.

In addition, find out everything you can about your daughter's boyfriend. Does he come from an abusive home? Has he ever been in trouble with the law? Is he on probation? If you have reason to believe that the boyfriend is abusive, find out if his parents are willing to discuss the relationship. If you are able to set up a meeting with them, bring a professional with you—your pastor, a counselor, or an abuse advocate. You may present your case to them. If abuse is suspected, talk with the parents about how their son treats women and express your concerns. Make it clear that you are going to protect your daughter. If the boy has already shown himself to be abusive, then be more direct. Tell the parents: "We are making every effort to protect our daughter and respectfully request that you explain this to your son so that we will not have to take legal action against him." If your daughter and her boyfriend are living together, do not contact her boyfriend or disclose any of the information that your daughter has passed on to you, as this could endanger her life. Abuse is based on power and control, so do not recommend couple counseling, either, as it will not stop the violence and could, in fact, cause it to escalate. In chapter 6 we will discuss various options and safety plans that you may implement if your daughter is living with or married to her abuser.

Discovering Your Resources

Often a parent's first instinct when learning of a daughter's violent boyfriend is to lock the door and keep the family inside. Don't do it. Seek help from others who have the knowledge and experience to guide you and your daughter to safety. At this point you may feel completely alone and without hope, but the resources are there for you to find.

Whom can you call for information, direction, and comfort? One, you can set up an appointment with your daughter's guidance counselor. Be sure that the appropriate school authorities are aware of the problem and your suspicions. Two, try making an appointment to talk with counselors at a local shelter for battered women. They'll be able to help you assess the situation and may recommend other resources. Don't forget to talk and pray with your pastor or a lay leader who is skilled in counseling.

Among Christians there is a tendency to focus on ways of keeping the family or couple together as opposed to seeking out options of safety for the battered victim. Some adults also view dating violence as nothing more than two kids playfully fighting and are unaware of the risks involved for the victim. If you feel that your church does not have a firm enough grasp on the dynamics of violence against women, then by all means trust your intuition and seek out the assistance of a caring adult who is aware of the many problems facing teens. Your options might include calling the council within your church district and requesting a list of clergy or lay persons that work specifically with these issues.

Steps to Safety

Once you have determined the extent of the abuse, begin immediately to find protection for your daughter. Her living situation and her response to your involvement will determine what kind of safety measures you may be able to pursue.

Your daughter may live at home and, like Sarah, welcome your intervention. If her abuser attends the same school, by all means alert the school authorities of the situation. Chances are, however, that the school will not be able to provide adequate protection. You may need to consider other educational options. Private school and boarding school are options, although costly ones. Short-term homeschooling, either by parents or a hired tutor, may be the best bet if she is willing to remain "cooped up" at home.

If you and she decide she should remain at home, help her to arrange safety plans that will allow her to lead as normal a life as possible. Encourage her friends to visit frequently. Ask responsible friends or relatives to accompany her to the mall or to school functions. Screen all calls with an answering machine and caller ID.

If your daughter no longer lives with you and has rejected your attempts to help her, don't give up. You may not be able to help her directly, but you do have access to people who can. If she won't listen to you, contact an adult she respects who would be willing to talk with her. Check with a local shelter or domestic abuse program. They may be able to suggest some ways to get her the help she needs. In chapter 7 I'll discuss the various legal actions you can take if the above options are not enough.

It is vital that you assess the problem carefully before deciding the best possible course of action for your family. By thoroughly evaluating your daughter's situation, you will be able to develop a plan that will work.

The Need for Intervention

Some counselors may disagree with the idea of removing or "rescuing" a teen from a violent relationship. When working with adult victims of abuse, we tend to offer empowerment options that allow them to make the final decision. This method gives control back to the victim and ultimately works in

> *Many young girls operate under tremendous peer pressure to have a boyfriend.*

her favor. But with young teenage girls, I am in favor of swift intervention that removes them from danger. Even if your daughter is rebellious, be firm about your expectations of her as a member of the family. Keep in mind that many young girls operate under tremendous peer pressure to have a boyfriend, often fearing rejection from their peers should they break off the relationship.

Violence has become an increasingly acceptable form of behavior in our society. Today's youth are inured to violence in a manner unique to this

generation.[23] Consequently, parenting now requires both love and intervention in order to keep
our children safe. We must help our teens to unlearn this tolerance toward violence as they learn to
develop equitable relationships.

Tammy's Story

A few years ago I counseled a seventeen-year-old
girl whose boyfriend had beaten her. The girl's
mother called me almost every day to see how her
daughter was getting along.

"Is Tammy making progress?" she asked.
"When do you think she'll be able to go on with her
life and put all of this behind her?"

I found myself walking on thin ice as I strug-
gled to protect Tammy's trust and confidence while
consoling her mother. Every week, Tammy entered
my office in a very depressed condition. Her psychiatrist had prescribed an antidepressant drug, but
most of the time Tammy seemed to be in another
world. One day, after many weeks of working with
Tammy, she opened up and shared her dreams with
me. It all started when I inadvertently mentioned
that my mother's physical therapist had canceled a
session. Suddenly Tammy poured out her desire to

become a physical therapist. A few years earlier, she had been in an automobile accident, and through physical therapy she had quickly recovered. From that moment on, Tammy's dream was to become a physical therapist. No one, however, had encouraged her to pursue this goal. As Tammy spoke of her desire to help others, her eyes began to shine and my own heart filled with hope.

"Have you told your mom and dad about this?" I asked excitedly.

Her face immediately fell.

"They wouldn't understand," she said. "My mom thinks that I can't do anything right. They think I'm stupid. I guess it's because I am stupid."

My heart went out to Tammy. Her description of her parents' lack of confidence in her abilities sounded all too true to me. My suspicions were confirmed when I spoke with Tammy's mother and carefully broached the topic of Tammy's academic future.

"Oh, Tammy could never make it into college," her mother said. "Her father and I feel that she just isn't smart enough to do anything other than child care or waitressing."

I was appalled by her remarks. According to the school guidance counselor, Tammy's IQ scores indicated that she was well above average and quite capable of realizing her dreams. I urged Tammy's mother to encourage her daughter by helping her to set up short-term scholastic goals that would raise her grades. She expressed mild interest and came by my office to pick up materials on various study methods. I soon found out that Tammy's mother was not at all responsive toward helping her daughter to excel. Instead, she wanted Tammy to finish high school as quickly as possible and enroll in a quick certificate program that would ensure her of a minimum-wage job.

Tammy had always been a trial to her parents. She had been in and out of trouble throughout most her life, and now she was recovering from a violent relationship. Yet the more I talked with her mother, the more I believed that Tammy's parents were largely responsible for her problems. They refused to encourage her, and Tammy's mother seemed bent on crushing her daughter's dreams by insisting that she get out of school quickly and leave home. I eventually lost touch with Tammy, but one of her friends told me that she had dropped out of school and was waiting tables at a restaurant. My prayer is that Tammy will stay out of future abusive relationships and someday return to school to pursue her dreams.

How many girls are held back by parents who will not take the time to become involved in their lives? Research indicates that two out of five women in the workforce are the sole providers for their families. Statistics reveal that in the first year after separation or divorce, a woman's standard of living drops by 73 percent, while a man's improves by an average of 42 percent.[24] Although domestic violence crosses all socioeconomic, religious, ethnic, and educational backgrounds, a large percentage of women remain entrenched in violent relationships

> *A girl who believes that Prince Charming will sweep her into Happily Ever After will enter relationships with a severe handicap.*

because they lack the financial resources to survive as a single parent. In addition, up to 50 percent of all homeless women and children in this nation are fleeing from domestic violence.[25]

A girl who is raised to believe that Prince Charming will someday sweep her off into Happily

Ever After will enter relationships with a severe handicap. What if her prince turns out to be an abuser? What if he dies or leaves her for a younger, more attractive princess? Will she have the skills to make a decent living on her own? A teen who prepares for a financially stable career will be a step further away from victimization.

Jesus said, "If you have faith as small as a mustard seed, you can say to this mountain, 'Move from here to there' and it will move. Nothing will be impossible for you" (Matthew 17:20). The hope and encouragement you try to give your battered daughter may seem no bigger than a mustard seed compared to the mountain of violence she has faced. But it will go a long way toward helping her to develop the assertiveness and self-confidence that will allow her to become the woman God created her to be.

Setting Realistic Goals

Once an abused teen has been able to sever her relationship with her abuser, she will need help in getting her life back together. Dating violence is a multidimensional problem. The abused teen may need to work toward several long-range goals. If she has dropped out of school due to pregnancy or depression, she may need to work toward a high school equivalency diploma. If she was seriously injured, she may be facing months of physical therapy. And dealing with the emotional and psychological trauma will most certainly require long-term effort.

When I work with a teen who has been battered by her boyfriend, I encourage her to make her long-term goals behaviorally specific. A nonspecific goal would be, "I want to start a new life." A behaviorally specific goal would necessitate defining that new life. She may define it like this: "I want to start a new life by getting my high school diploma so that I can go to college and then law school. I want to help abused children and teens."

Next, we work on establishing short-term goals that would help her achieve her long-term goal. For example: "I will join a program that will help me study for a high school equivalency exam," "I will volunteer at a domestic abuse shelter," or "I will pass my GED and apply for college." Breaking down her goals into small steps will help her to see her future with clarity and hope.

Dating violence does not have to lead to tragedy. Whatever your daughter's situation may be, whatever phase of abuse the relationship is in, there is hope. You may wish to skip ahead to chapters 7 and 8, where you'll find legal information and an extensive list of resources that will assist you in planning your intervention.

5

Prevention: Raising Assertive Daughters and Sons

A popular TV commercial urges parents to make an appointment with their teens to discuss the danger of drugs. While this is a good idea, it certainly points out that many parents today are too busy to talk with their children about important issues—so they have to be reminded to make an appointment to do it. We live in a world where often both parents must hold down full-time employment. Families are more mobile; kids no longer have a grandparent or other relative nearby to care for them.

A rigid work schedule can make it difficult for you to spend generous amounts of time with your daughter. I can assure you, however, that the more that you involve yourself in her activities, hopes, and dreams, the less likely she will be to wander into a potentially lethal relationship. While you ultimately may not be able to prevent your daughter from becoming involved in an abusive relationship, your appropriate nurturing and support are invaluable to her and should begin long before she enters adolescence.

Looking Ahead

I believe that in order for teenage girls to develop the sense of power and self-worth that is necessary for avoiding abusive relationships, parents must encourage their daughters to set their sights on a prize they wish to gain. Girls have to live with achievable goals in mind.

One of the first steps is to identify your daughter's motivation. What are her long-term and short-term goals? What does she dream of accomplishing one day? Are her goals reflective of her strengths and interests? You may find that your daughter is unsure of her strengths and talents. Now is the time for a booster shot of self-confidence. Remember

Tammy? I believe Tammy could have turned her life completely around if her parents had, first of all, looked beyond her behavior to find her interests, strengths, and gifts, and, secondly, encouraged her to pursue her goal of becoming a physical therapist.

Another step to help your daughter—or your son—to grow up with healthy self esteem is to create a home environment that empowers children. Although each parent/child relationship is unique, firmness with openness and increasing freedom seems to be helpful. Child psychologist Diana Baumrind in her paper "Early Socialization and Adolescent Competence," cites three distinct patterns of parenting.[26]

> *Authoritative parents are firm but understanding, setting limits while encouraging independence.*

Authoritarian parents are rigid, punitive, and unsympathetic. They value obedience from their children and authority for themselves. Authoritarian parents try to curb their child's will and shape their child's behavior to meet a set standard. They are detached and seldom praise their youngsters. Authoritarian parents may try to define their child's goal themselves.

Authoritative parents use reasoning skills with their children and encourage give-and-take, allowing them increased responsibility as they become older. Authoritative parents are firm but understanding, setting limits while encouraging independence. Their demands are reasonable, rational, and consistent. Authoritative parents walk with their child as he or she seeks to identify goals.

Permissive parents give their children great freedom, and their discipline is lax. Some permissive parents are simply uninvolved in their children's lives. Others give their children unconditional encouragement and support but without guidelines or structure to help them make good choices. Permissive parents stand on the sidelines and cheer (or not) as their child wanders around looking for a goal to seek.

Take some time to analyze your own parenting style. Do you fall clearly into one of the three categories? In what ways have you adapted your parenting style to your child's personality? If you feel uneasy about any aspects of your parenting style, talk with your spouse and possibly your pastor or a counselor.

Approaching the Gate

Running the race of life requires lifelong training. Just as an athlete learns how to breathe, how to move, and when to speed up or slow down, a young person learns the best techniques for his or her life journey. Teaching your daughter to set healthy boundaries could help to prevent her from being drawn into an abusive relationship. Most men have absolutely no difficulty in saying no. Women, on the other hand, often feel guilty about using the *N* word. Many battered teens are limited in their ability to set healthy boundaries for themselves.

In their struggle for independence, teens tend to look on parental rules as fences designed to keep them from experiencing life. Often it takes a few bad experiences before a teen realizes that those fences also keep the bad things out. Talk with your daughter frequently about the importance of positive and healthy relationships. Model in your own marriage the caring and give-and-take that are characteristic of strong marriages. Be very clear about your own values, but don't lecture.

Know your children's friends and their parents. Supervise your teens as much as possible by establishing house rules and curfews early in their development, modifying the rules as they become older. Many teens are relieved to be able to use parental rules as an excuse to get out of an uncomfortable situation. Knowing that your children can take care of themselves when things get out of hand will take some of the sting out of being the "bad guy"!

Do not allow your daughter to date at an early age; young teens (thirteen to fifteen) may encounter risky situations that they may be too emotionally immature to handle. I further suggest that parents not allow their daughters to date boys who are significantly older—perhaps two or three years—than the girls. Although older boys are particularly glamorous to young girls, especially if they have a car, the power differences can create precarious situations.

Doing your best as a parent will frequently entail finding a balance between actively participating in your daughter's life and knowing when to back off and let her fly. In all circumstances, parenting should always involve supporting healthy choices and promoting firm boundaries.

Eyes on the Prize

Ben's fourteen-year-old daughter, Rachel, is a walking pendulum. One minute she's planning her acceptance speech for the Oscars. The next minute she's in front of the mirror, wailing, "They'll never pick me for the school play! My hair is the wrong color, I'm too fat, and nobody at school has as many zits as I have!"

Even teens who rocket out of the starting gate, heading straight for the prize (their goal), can be slowed down by self-doubt. That self-doubt can origi-nate from the conflict between their own gifts and what society values. Our society values the superficial. The next time you're in the supermarket, compare the number of magazines devoted to fashion, beauty, and fitness with those that deal with intellectual and spiri-tual pursuits. If you zero in on the teen magazines, you'll find the ratio even more extreme.

Take every opportunity to praise your daugh-ter's inner beauty. Compliment her on her ideas, her insights, her social skills: "It was really nice of you to call Carrie after she lost her job"; "I'm im-pressed that you noticed I've been stressed-out lately. Thanks for your concern"; "That's an interest-ing idea you have about helping the homeless. Let's talk about it." Point out positive role models. Look for women athletes who uphold strong values, or popular singers who show compassion and con-cern for others.

By all means continue to compliment your daughter on her appearance. But target the things that reflect her skills and her sense of self: "That outfit looks great. The colors you chose really complement each other"; "You look so poised today. You must be feeling good about yourself."

Assertive vs. Aggressive

Assertiveness-training courses and self-defense for women are found in most community centers, colleges, and adult-education programs these days. Both women and girls can learn to defend themselves against assault and to maintain their rights in the workplace. But when was the last time you saw an assertiveness-training course for men? I can hear many of my gender laughing: "Since when do men need to learn to be assertive?"

For many, the terms *assertive* and *aggressive* seem to be synonymous. In fact, they are not. Understanding the differences between assertiveness and aggression is crucial for parents seeking to raise daughters and sons who are courageous and kind, strong and selfless, and sure of their place and their purpose in the world.

Roget's Thesaurus offers a number of synonyms for the words *assertive* and *aggressive:*

assured	attacking
certain	combative
confident	destructive
decisive	intrusive
emphatic	offensive
positive	quarrelsome
self-assured	threatening
self-confident	warlike

I'm sure you had no trouble deciding which words describe assertive and which describe aggressive. How often, however, have you heard women who display the characteristics in the lefthand column

> *The prevalence of abuse would be greatly reduced if boys in our society were taught to be assertive rather than aggressive.*

described as aggressive? Would a man who displayed the same characteristics be called aggressive?

Women in our society have made considerable

progress in the past few decades toward regaining our voice, our strength, and our self-assurance as persons of value. I would like to suggest, however, that the prevalence of dating and domestic abuse would be greatly reduced if boys in our society were also taught to be assertive rather than aggressive.

Abuse Begets Abuse

One of my colleagues recently told me that in all the years that he had provided treatment to abusers, he could only recall a small number of battering males who had not been raised by an abusive father or stepfather. According to the National Coalition Against Domestic Violence, males who witnessed their parents' acts of violence are three times more likely to abuse their own wives or girlfriends.[27]

It is not at all unusual for the young children of a battered mother to behave violently; this is what they have observed in the home. When clients with young sons come to me for advocacy or counseling, I have frequently seen these children behaving aggressively toward their mothers even as we talk. I remember a little boy saying, "Mommy, don't talk to her!" and slapping his mother across the arm. This little boy's attempt at control was a direct result of seeing his father forbid his wife to talk to friends and relatives. The child knew from experience that when his mother went against his father's wishes, she received a beating. The boy may have actually been trying to protect his mother from his father's wrath. But the only way he knew to control her behavior was with violence.

I'll never forget one four year old who was taken aback when I told him to stop hitting his mother. He replied, "That's what my daddy does, and I'll smack your mouth if you don't shut up!" I firmly told him that he was not to talk to me in that manner, and I reassured him of his safe surroundings by talking and playing with him until our child therapist arrived.

Sadly, these little boys not only abuse their mothers, but they also frequently turn on their sisters. On the surface these boys may seem like spoiled brats in need of discipline, but for those of us who observe this behavior on a daily basis, we know that we are seeing a future girlfriend—or wife—beater. Over the past few years, I have started seeing the battered girlfriends of the young men who came through our shelter program with their mothers a few years ago. I have no doubt that battering is a learned behavior.

Real Men Don't . . .

An abusive family is not the only contributor to the proliferation of dating abuse. Just as women are

> **Boys who watched violent shows were more likely than those who watched nonviolent shows to behave aggressively.**

portrayed in the media as dolls and playthings, men are depicted as self-centered slackers, bullies, and cutthroat businessmen ruled by greed and hormones. Whatever happened to the sensitive guy?

In one television study, groups of boys watched violent or nonviolent programs in a controlled setting and then played floor hockey.[28] Boys who had watched the violent shows were more likely than those who had watched nonviolent shows to behave aggressively on the hockey floor. The effect was greatest in boys who displayed aggressive tendencies to begin with. Another study, this one done internationally, tracked people from age eight, in 1960, until age thirty, in 1982.[29] The results indicated that those who watched more TV violence as children were significantly more likely to be convicted of violent crimes, to produce aggressive children, and to rely on physical punishment in raising those children. Countries such as Finland, which carries few violent programs on television, had a much lower percentage of aggressive behaviors.

The Assertive Male

I believe there are several things that parents and churches can do to prevent young men from engaging in abusive behavior. Churches are especially well equipped to help with this task because Jesus is the perfect role model. Organizations such as the conservative men's group, Promise Keepers, often get a bad rap by the media and some women's groups. Men who attend these functions, however, seem to come away with a renewed spirit and a positive attitude toward the women in their lives. For this reason, boys should be given ample opportunity to attend such outings with their church groups. Pastors might also make an extra effort to include teens and young men in their Bible studies and prayer breakfasts. The sons of single mothers would especially benefit from these opportunities.

Professional sports in the U.S. are becoming more sensationalistic and violent every year. Parents need to identify and hold up as role models those rare athletes who demonstrate integrity. Also, observe other parents as they interact with their sons. What parenting techniques seem to inspire cooperation, kindness, selflessness, and self-confidence? What parenting techniques seem to encourage insensitivity and aggression? If you are the parent of both a son and a daughter, compare the ways you interact with them. What do you expect from your daughter? What do you expect from your son? If the expectations are different, what are the reasons for that?

Boys who are raised to be assertive rather than aggressive will be much less likely to engage in violent behavior. By the same token, girls who are raised to be assertive rather than passive will be much less likely to allow themselves to be drawn into an abusive relationship. A boy and a girl who respect themselves and each other will enjoy a relationship that is beneficial to both for however long it lasts. What more could a parent hope for?

6

When Your Daughter Marries Her Abuser

J ennifer King was just out of high school when she decided to travel to South America for the summer with a missionary group from her church. Jennifer's parents were thrilled by their daughter's desire to serve God as a missionary. Many of Jennifer's friends had dropped out of church, so the Kings were pleased that their only child had remained committed to her faith.

During the mission trip, Jennifer met Mark, a young, dynamic youth pastor who had accompanied the group. The two fell madly in love, and before the summer had ended they were married. Jennifer's parents were very disappointed that she did not tell them about the engagement. Moreover, they had wanted her to complete her education before getting married. Yet in spite of the fact that Jennifer was only eighteen while her new husband was twenty-six, the Kings were impressed with Mark's ministry. They had no other option but to trust that Jennifer had made the right decision. So they supported Jennifer and Mark in their marriage and even helped them financially.

When You Get a Call to the ER

At first Jennifer's parents didn't notice anything out of the ordinary. They did not get to see her very often, but they credited her rare visits to the fact that she and Mark were newlyweds and wanted to spend as much time together as possible. Then one evening, only six months after the wedding, the Kings received a startling phone call from the police advising them to get to the hospital as quickly as possible—their daughter had been in an accident. When they arrived at the hospital, they were totally unprepared for what they found. Mark, in a fit of rage, had pushed Jennifer out of the car, leaving her for dead on the side of a busy highway. Fortunately, she had sustained far fewer injuries than one might expect.

Jennifer's parents were stunned that their charming son-in-law could have done such a thing. Jennifer admitted that Mark had been violent on several occasions. Once he had even locked her in a closet for several hours because she offered to sing at a church function without first asking his permission.

The Kings had no idea what to do to help their daughter. Their first mistake was to arrange a counseling session for Jennifer and Mark with their pastor. Marital counseling is a noxious remedy for victims of domestic violence.[30] In order for any type of counseling to be effective, there must be equality and honesty between the partners involved. Because battering is a control issue and not a communication problem,

> *After the second counseling session, Jennifer ended up in the emergency room with a broken arm.*

counseling poses a major threat to the abuser's power over his victim. Consequently, after each session, violence tends to escalate.

After the second counseling session, Jennifer ended up in the emergency room with a broken arm. Apparently Mark felt that Jennifer had said too much during their second meeting with the counselor. In that particular session, Jennifer had felt "safe" enough to openly share about some of her husband's violent patterns of behavior. Their pastor, knowing nothing of the abuse, was shocked. When they arrived home after the counseling session, Mark exploded at Jennifer for embarrassing him in front of his senior pastor.

When the pastor found out that Mark had injured Jennifer after the session, he called them both into his office and reprimanded Mark for his behavior. At the same time, however, he also told Jennifer that she should be more patient with her husband and make a greater effort not to "set him off." Instead of privately confronting Mark and referring him to a specialized treatment program for abusers, the pastor unwittingly made Jennifer responsible for the abuse. Mark was angry with his pastor, but he feared losing his position at the church. So he backed off and left Jennifer alone for several weeks.

During the sessions that followed, Mark alleged that their problems were caused by the intrusiveness of Jennifer's parents. Of course by now,

Jennifer had learned the hard way that unless Mark remained in total control of the counseling sessions, she would suffer severe repercussions. So she agreed with whatever he said, even though she knew it wasn't true. The pastor suggested that Jennifer ask her parents to back off so that they might have more time to work on their marriage. This gave Mark the necessary ammunition for further isolating Jennifer.

Jennifer's mother, Elizabeth, came to see me after Jennifer's third trip to the hospital. She had heard about our local domestic violence program from a friend and thought that I might be able to help.

"Mark seemed like such a nice young man," Elizabeth said. "He still seems that way at church—even though Ted and I know what he's capable of. If only they hadn't gotten married. I feel like we've lost our daughter forever."

The Kings had raised their daughter in a loving, Christian environment where she had been free to express her artistic talents as a singer. They had supported Jennifer in all of her endeavors throughout her life, and in turn, she had never given them any of the typical teenage problems. When some of her classmates became involved in drugs, Jennifer quietly made new friends. Although two girls had become pregnant in high school, Jennifer did not become sexually active until after her marriage to Mark.

After several conversations with Elizabeth, however, I discovered that she and her husband had never talked to their daughter about the importance of becoming an independent young woman. Jennifer's parents had filled her head with visions of a nice young man who would marry her and "take care of everything." Mark used the Bible as a weapon, casting verses about submission at Jennifer until her self-esteem plummeted and she began to believe that maybe she deserved the abuse.

Professionals in the field of domestic violence are aware that females with low self-esteem and submissive personalities are far more likely to become caught up in a violent relationship. We live in a world where very few young men have been taught the true meaning of spiritual leadership, and due to this, violence against women is at an all-time high.

Submission vs. Abuse

Submission and male headship remain somewhat volatile issues among conservative Christians. I do not presume to know all of the answers regarding God's plan for men and women. Many families are able to function beautifully by a hierarchical standard of male headship and female submission, while other homes are filled with cruelty and domination based on the same model. Marriage vows were never intended to involve partners in violent relationships. The image of marriage given to us in the Bible is that of Jesus' giving himself for the church. Paul clearly states that men are to love their wives as Christ loved the church and gave himself for her (Ephesians 5:25).

Elizabeth soon realized that even though Jennifer was married, she and Ted could not stand by and do nothing. So we began to discuss safety plans for Jennifer. During our planning sessions we focused on various strategies through which they could support Jennifer without Mark's being aware of it. These plans not only helped to keep Jennifer alive; they also empowered her parents by giving them hope.

Step one of our plan entailed Elizabeth's calling her daughter while Mark wasn't home. Through this phone call she would convey her love and unconditional support. This would not be an easy task; Mark insisted that his wife be at his side almost all of the time. But Elizabeth remembered that on Saturday afternoons Mark took his youth group on outings, and Jennifer was seldom allowed to attend. So Elizabeth called her daughter the next Saturday afternoon to let her know that she and Jennifer's father would always be there for her, no matter what. Jennifer was happy to hear from her mother and confided to her that she desperately needed help. Mark had become so controlling that Jennifer seldom had even one moment to herself. It was an emotional and difficult conversation for both of them. Elizabeth later told me, however, that the phone call to Jennifer was the most positive step that she had taken since discovering the violence.

"When I told Jennifer I'd be there for her no matter what, that's exactly what I meant," Elizabeth said. "I just want my daughter to live, and if I can somehow keep her alive until she has the presence of mind to leave Mark, then that's exactly what I intend to do."

For Jennifer, this first step meant everything. She now knew that she could return to her parents' home, even for a short time if necessary. She could give Mark time to cool off without fear of letting anyone down.

On the following Saturday afternoon while

Mark was out with his youth group, the Kings implemented step two of the plan. They drove to Jennifer's home and gave her a cell phone to use for

> *Jennifer's father made arrangements with a taxi service that agreed to pick Jennifer up without advance charge.*

emergencies. Now, even if Mark pulled the phone out of the wall in a fit of rage, Jennifer could call for help. She frequently hid from Mark in the basement of their home, mainly because there was a secure lock on the door. I suggested that she hide the cell phone behind the freezer, keeping it charged at all times. Meanwhile, Jennifer's father made arrangements with a taxi service that agreed to pick Jennifer up without advance charge. If Jennifer was too afraid or embarrassed to call 911, she could call the taxi service, and they would send her parents the bill. The Kings also gave their daughter a credit card for emergency use.

Jennifer hid the credit card and cell phone in the basement with an emergency escape kit—an overnight case with clothes and necessities for a few days in case she were forced to leave home. Elizabeth programmed both the cab service and 911 into the cell phone so that Jennifer only had to remember one digit, making the entire procedure simple to carry out in a crisis.

Elizabeth and I worked on backup plans. We drew a map of Jennifer and Mark's house, indicating emergency exits in case Jennifer could not make it to the basement. Elizabeth had extra sets of keys made for her daughter's car and hid them in strategic locations throughout the house and the yard.

Soon Jennifer began to call her parents more often, and she felt free to leave when Mark began showing signs of violent behavior. On several occasions Jennifer did use her escape route and went to her parents' house for a few days. Once she stayed away from Mark for several weeks, only to return home when he promised that he would change. Ted King took a strong stand with Mark and told him that he could not visit Jennifer when she was seeking shelter with them. During the honeymoon phase of the relationship, Jennifer's parents remained steadfast in their support of Jennifer, telling her that she should stick to her safety plan and call if she needed them. They avoided telling her what she should or should not do, but they bluntly reminded her about the danger she was in. The Kings never wavered in their support of their daughter, and never said "I told you so" when Jennifer called them in a crisis.

Eventually, Mark beat Jennifer severely enough that when she dialed 911 the police came to their home and arrested him. He was charged with assault and spent several weeks in jail before being ordered by a judge to participate in a treatment program for domestic abusers. Meanwhile, Jennifer's father went to Mark's pastor, telling him that Mark needed serious spiritual intervention as well. Their pastor agreed, and the church council ordered Mark to step down from his position as youth pastor. They agreed to reconsider their decision if at some point Mark could prove that he had changed his behavior. During the twenty-four months of intense counseling and weekly group therapy, Mark began to unlearn much of his violent behavior—behavior that had been passed on to him by his own father. Jennifer and Mark were eventually reunited, and the physical abuse stopped. But Jennifer has told her mother that Mark is still verbally abusive from time to time, and she does not know how much longer she'll remain with him.

Marriage Commitment vs. Physical Safety

The recovery rate for batterers is quite low.[31] One reason is that abusers have a tendency to blame their problem on other people, specifically their victims. Elizabeth still worries about her daughter, but she realizes that Jennifer feels bound to Mark through their marriage vows. Many battered young women remain in abusive relationships because of their strong convictions about the sanctity of marriage. Their righteous values are laudable. But also misguided. Are battered women supposed to forgive and forget and move back with the batterer?

Jesus said: "Take heed to yourselves; if your brother sins, rebuke him, and if he repents, forgive him; and if he sins against you seven times in the day, and turns to you seven times, and says, 'I repent,' you must forgive him" (Luke 17:3-4, RSV). The Reverend Marie Fortune in her book *Keeping the Faith* points out that we tend to overlook some of the most important parts of these verses.[32] The first is that we are to take care ("take heed") of ourselves. Then, if someone abuses us, we rebuke him. We confront him with his wrong behavior. After that, if he repents, then we forgive him.

"Repentance here means more than remorse," Fortune writes. "Remorse is when he says, 'I'm really sorry, honey. I didn't mean to hurt you. It'll never happen again.' Repentance is much more significant. To repent, in both Old and New Testaments, means to turn away from, to change, never to repeat again."[33]

Of course, some would argue still that a woman must not divorce her abuser. We cannot get into the thorny theological issues here, but surely God would not have a woman stay in a situation where she is continually abused. She must be safe, whether she pursues divorce or not. The Bible does not condone unjustified violence.

Elizabeth now battles with her own guilt for not teaching Jennifer to be more assertive, but she can be proud of making every attempt to intercept the violence. By focusing on safety issues, Elizabeth was able to keep Jennifer alive until she was ready to end the marriage or until Mark sought help. The Kings also encouraged Jennifer to contact domestic violence counselors, providing her with hotline crisis numbers. Jennifer later told her mother that she had often called the hotline when depressed and in need of someone who would listen without knowing who she was.

If your daughter is married to an abuser, this

does not mean that she is beyond your grasp. For one thing, because she is married, she can take refuge in a shelter and seek help through legal and social channels that are not available to unmarried teens. Like the Kings, you can take a number of actions to provide for her safety. The next chapter and the appendix contain specific information on people and programs that are qualified to assist both you and your daughter.

7 *Getting Help*

In 1973 in Stockholm, Sweden, two thieves held several people hostage in a bank for six days. During these six days, an unbelievable thing happened. The hostages began to bond with their captors. Because the prisoners depended on the thieves for their survival, they began to care for the two men and try to find ways to help them. Professional negotiators now call this phenomenon the "Stockholm syndrome."

Teens and young women who have endured long-term abuse from their boyfriends may experience a similar phenomenon. Psychologists believe that repeated assaults can cause severe psychological distress and dysfunction, cognitive changes in how the battered girl views herself and the world, and even dissociative disorders. The battered teen may feel sorry for her abuser and make every effort to protect him from her parents and law enforcement. This is commonly referred to as "traumatic bonding." If you suspect your daughter's abuse is psychologically severe, seek help from a professional.

Seeking Help

There are several criteria you may consider when seeking the help of a professional counselor. Not every mental health professional is appropriate for your daughter's special needs. If she is still in the relationship and does not feel she can get out, I suggest that you keep her focused on ways that she can remain safe, while directing her toward a therapist who understands the dynamics of partner abuse. Call your local domestic violence program for referrals. (Your physician, hospital emergency room, or community mental health agency should have numbers.) Many domestic violence agencies employ licensed professional counselors who are available at minimal or no charge. Counseling services are also available through mental-health programs and family-service agencies.

When selecting a counselor, do not hesitate to inquire about his or her experience and training in the dynamics of domestic violence and battered women. If the counselor does not appear interested in your inquiries or seems to possess little knowledge in the area of your concern, look elsewhere. Find out what techniques the counselor uses when treating victims of dating abuse. Make absolutely certain that the counselor you choose does *not* practice couple counseling when abuse is present in a relationship. Finally, be sure the counselor or an appropriate substitute will be available in the middle of the night or on weekends in case an emergency should arise.

Addiction can also play a major role in keeping a victim dependent upon her abuser. Many teens are introduced to drugs and alcohol through an abusive boyfriend.

Evelyn was only seventeen when her boyfriend introduced her to crack cocaine. She wanted to leave her boyfriend but was unable to make the break simply because she was addicted and afraid of withdrawal from the drugs. After two years of abuse, Evelyn's parents finally talked her into a drug rehabilitation hospital for treatment.

"One morning I woke up and decided that I'd had enough," she said. "I was only nineteen, but I felt as if my life was over. From the moment that Bobby introduced me to drugs, I had been on a roller-coaster ride of beatings and drug abuse. So, before I had time to change my mind, I called my dad and begged him to get me into a hospital. By the end of the day I was in a drug rehabilitation hospital, and after staying there for three months I went into a shelter. Drugs most definitely kept me in the abusive relationship. Between the beatings and the crack, I'm lucky to be alive."

Taking Legal Action

Sometimes the only way to rescue a victim from abuse is by taking legal action. Every state offers some sort of civil remedy in the form of a restraining order to assist victims of domestic violence. Temporary orders that restrain the abuser generally last seven to ten days until a hearing is set. After a hearing, the order can become permanent and remain in effect for a year or longer. If the abuser violates this order by stalking, calling, threatening, or harassing the victim in any manner, then he can be placed under arrest and spend time in jail or juvenile detention. He may be ordered by a judge to attend a different school and seek counseling. In many states, including my own state of North Carolina, if an abuser violates a civil order, his behavior automatically becomes a misdemeanor, which is a criminal offense.

The law can be a very effective tool in stopping domestic violence. If the abusive teen knows that his violence may land him in jail or prevent him from furthering his education, then he might back off, especially if he is stalking his girlfriend or making threats. Of course, every abusive situation carries its own unique set of circumstances, and in some cases, the abuser will not back off no matter how many times he is warned.

Some battered teens may fear that taking criminal action against the boyfriend will only aggravate him, making the situation worse. Clearly, there are positive and negative elements involved in making a decision to take legal action. A restraining order will not provide your daughter with an armed guard to protect her on a twenty-four-hour basis. If the abuser is totally unwilling to comply with the order, then your daughter may be placed in a higher risk category. This is why safety planning for the victim is always a crucial part of any legal response.

The positive component of legal action is that it enhances the ability of law enforcement to make an arrest if the abuser continues to make threats. If your daughter has a restraining order in effect and her boyfriend threatens her, the police may be able to arrest him immediately, before he harms her. Without an order, the police cannot make an arrest unless the abuser has physically harmed the victim.

Laws vary from state to state, but in order to find out exactly what the law is concerning your situation, you could contact the following agencies for information and referral:

> **Local legal aid services** offer general legal information free of charge. In some cases, legal-aid staff attorneys will assist clients in obtaining a restraining order through the court system. Some states require victims of domestic violence to be eighteen or over and residing with the abuser before an order can be issued, but many states will issue these orders to minors with the consent of an adult or guardian. Legal aid will be able to point you in the right direction. Check the social service listings in your telephone book, or ask at a women's shelter or bar association.
>
> **The district attorney's office** can provide information on how to prosecute and can refer you to the appropriate people.
>
> **Your local police chief, sheriff, or magis-**

trate is often the first one to turn to in your area. He or she will know what channels to follow and may be able to bring in outside assistance.

Domestic violence programs and mental health agencies may offer a host of services, including twenty-four-hour crisis lines, short-term counseling, and, in some cases, emergency housing. Your daughter may require a wide range of services to deal with the after-effects of dating violence. Having access to as many resources as possible is essential for the most effective handling of her needs. A victim of dating violence who is supported emotionally is far more likely to bear up under the stress of seeking temporary shelter, changing schools, or pursuing legal investigations. The appendix contains names, addresses, and phone numbers of organizations that specialize in dealing with domestic and dating abuse.

Community efforts to address domestic violence have expanded greatly, especially over the last twenty years. Comprehensive community-based task forces have sprung up all over the nation with an emphasis on expanded legal protection, housing, and health care for battered women. But to date, we have few services for teens who are faced with the same dilemma as their adult counterparts. Teens often cannot avail themselves of services for adult women unless they are accompanied by a parent.

I hope that it is not idealistic to think that over the next decade we will see safe houses that are designed specifically for battered teens, along with programs that address their needs for healing, expanded legal services, and full recovery of their self-esteem. But this dream can only come true through the concerted efforts of individuals devoted to improving the lives of those who are caught in the grip of teen dating violence—individuals such as parents, pastors, counselors, teachers, and friends who develop an understanding of the dangers and become familiar with the warning signs and the correct responses to teen abuse.

Appendix A

Are You Dating an Abusive Male?

Questions for Girls

You may be involved in an abusive relationship if your boyfriend . . .

- ❖ Constantly ignores your feelings

- ❖ Has ridiculed or insulted women as a group

- ❖ Insults your most valued beliefs or friends

- ❖ Threatens to hurt you or your family

- ❖ Degrades you in private but is charming in public

- ❖ Abused his former girlfriend

- ❖ Threatens to abuse you

- ❖ Punches, kicks, or exerts physical control over you

❖ Has prevented you from leaving his presence

❖ Has threatened you with the use of weapons

If you are involved in an abusive relationship . . .

❖ Believe in yourself! It is quite common for you to feel as though the abuse was your fault. This is because boys who abuse their girlfriends have a tendency to blame them for the problem instead of taking responsibility for their own behavior. Abuse is never the fault of the victim!

❖ If you fear that you will be harmed by your boyfriend, seek shelter from a friend or domestic violence program.

❖ Talk about it! Contact a friend or one of the help lines listed in Appendix B.

Relationships are an important part of life and a bad one could destroy your chances for a bright future. Avoid boys who . . .

❖ Use drugs or alcohol or make derogatory statements about women

❖ Want to be in control of where you go and what you do

❖ Enjoy pornography

❖ Keep track of your time

❖ Expect you to look and act a certain way

❖ Are overly jealous or possessive

Appendix B

Domestic Violence Resources for Families

While many of the numbers listed for the organizations below are centralized, they will almost always be able to refer the caller to a local agency.

State Domestic Violence Agencies

Alabama Coalition Against Domestic Violence
205-832-4842

Alaska Network on Domestic Violence and Sexual Assault
907-586-3650

Arizona Coalition Against Domestic Violence
602-279-2900

Arizona Toll-Free Hotline
800-782-6400

Arkansas Coalition Against Violence to Women
501-663-4668

California (Southern) Coalition on Battered Women
213-655-6098

California (Northern and Central) Coalition on
    Battered Women
209-524-1888

Colorado Domestic Violence Coalition
303-573-9018

Connecticut Coalition Against Domestic Abuse
203-524-5890

Delaware Domestic Violence Task Force
303-762-6110

D.C. Coalition Against Domestic Abuse
202-783-5332

Florida Spouse Abuse, Inc.
407-886-2856

Florida Coalition Against Domestic Violence
904-668-6862

Florida-Toll Free Hotline
800-500-1119

Georgia Advocates for Battered Women and
    Children
404-524-3847
Georgia Toll-Free Hotline
800-643-1212

Georgia Coalition on Battered Women
404-870-9612

Hawaii State Committee for Family Violence
808-486-5072

Idaho Coalition Against Domestic Violence and
Sexual Assault
203-384-0419

Illinois Coalition Against Domestic Violence
217-789-2830

Indiana Coalition Against Domestic Violence
317-543-3908

Iowa Coalition Against Domestic Violence
515-281-7284

Kansas Coalition Against Domestic Violence
and Sexual Assault
913-232-9784

Kentucky Domestic Violence Association
502-875-4132

Louisiana Coalition Against Domestic Violence
504-542-4446

Maine Coalition for Family Crisis Services
207-941-1194

Maryland Network Against Domestic Violence
301-942-0900

Massachusetts Coalition of Battered Women's
Service Groups
617-248-0922

Michigan Coalition Against Domestic Violence
517-484-2924

Minnesota Coalition for Battered Women
621-646-6177

Mississippi Coalition Against Domestic Violence
601-436-3809

Missouri Coalition Against Domestic Violence
314-634-4161

Montana Coalition Against Domestic Violence
406-256-6334

Nebraska Domestic Violence & Sexual Assault
Coalition
402-476-6256

Nevada Network Against Domestic Violence
702-358-1171

Nevada Toll-Free Hotline
800-500-1556

New Hampshire Coalition Against Domestic
Violence & Sexual Assault
603-224-8893

New Hampshire Toll-Free Hotline
800-853-3388

New Jersey Coalition for Battered Women
609-584-8107

New Jersey Toll-Free Hotline
800-572-7233

New Mexico Coalition Against Domestic Violence
505-246-9240

New Mexico Toll-Free Hotline
800-773-3645

New York State Coalition Against Domestic
  Violence
518-432-4864

New York Toll-Free Hotline (English)
800-942-6906

New York Toll-Free Hotline (Spanish)
800-942-6908

North Carolina Coalition Against Domestic
  Violence
919-956-9124

North Dakota Council on Abused Women's
  Services
701-255-6240

North Dakota Toll-Free Hotline
800-472-2911

Ohio Domestic Violence Network
614-784-0023

Ohio Toll-Free Hotline
800-934-9840

Action Ohio Coalition for Battered Women
614-221-1255

Oklahoma Coalition on Domestic Violence and
   Sexual Assault
405-557-1210

Oklahoma Toll-Free Hotline
800-522-9054

Oregon Coalition Against Domestic Violence &
   Sexual Assault
503-223-7411

Pennsylvania Coalition Against Domestic Violence
717-545-6400

Pennsylvania Toll-Free Hotline
800-932-4632

Rhode Island Council on Domestic Violence
401-467-9940

Rhode Island Toll-Free Hotline
800-434-8100

South Carolina Coalition Against Domestic
Violence
803-254-3699

South Dakota Coalition Against Domestic Violence
605-225-5122

Tennessee Task Force Against Family Violence
615-327-0805

Tennessee Toll-Free Hotline
800-356-6767

Texas Council on Family Violence
512-794-1133

Utah Domestic Violence Advisory Council
801-538-4100

Vermont Network Against Domestic Violence &
Sexual Assault
802-223-1302

Virginians Against Domestic Violence
804-221-0990

Virginia Toll-Free Hotline
800-838-8238

Washington State Coalition Against Domestic
Violence
206-352-4029

Washington State Toll-Free Hotline
800-562-6025

West Virginia Coalition Against Domestic Violence
304-765-2250

Wisconsin Coalition Against Woman Abuse
608-255-0539

Wyoming Coalition on Family Violence & Sexual
   Assault
307-235-2814

Appendix C

National Domestic Violence Hotline/Resource Numbers (U.S.)

National Clearinghouse for the Defense of
   Battered Women
125 South 9th Street
Suite 302
Philadelphia, PA 19107
215-351-0010

National Coalition Against Domestic Violence
303-839-1852

National Domestic Violence Hotline
800-799-SAFE

National Organization of Victim's Assistance
   (NOVA)
202-232-6682

Reconstructive Surgery for Domestic Violence
   Victims
800-842-4546 (consultation & referral)

In Canada:
National Clearinghouse on Family Violence,
    Health, and Welfare
613-957-2938

In Puerto Rico:
Puerto Rico Comision para los Asuntos de la Mujer
1-809-722-2907

In the Virgin Islands:
Women's Resource Center—St. Thomas
809-776-3966

Women's Coalition of St. Croix
809-773-9272

Appendix D

Miscellaneous Resources for Parents and Teens

Advocates for Youth
(referrals and information on teen pregnancy)
1025 Vermont Avenue, NW
Suite 200
Washington, DC 20005
202-347-5700

Alcohol Hotline
(information and referral to local support always
    available)
800-ALCOHOL

American Association of Pastoral Counselors
9504-A Lee Highway
Fairfax, VA 22031
703-385-6967

Center for Disease Control National AIDS Hotline
800-342-2437 (English)
800-344-7432 (Spanish)
800-243-7889 (hearing impaired TTY/TDD)

Center for Disease Control AIDS Information
Clearinghouse
800-458-5231 (English/Spanish/French)
800-243-7012 (hearing impaired TTY/TDD)
(providing twenty-four-hour consultation,
information, referral, and educational material)

Cocaine Hotline
800-262-2463 (800-COCAINE)

Committee on the Status of Women
Women in Mission and Ministry Office
The Episcopal Church Center
815 Second Avenue
New York, NY 10017
800-334-7626

Child Help National Child-Abuse Hotline
800-422-4453
(hearing impaired)
800-2-A-Child

Covenant House Hotline for Problem Teens and
Runaways
800-999-9999

Men Stopping Violence
1020 Dekalb Avenue #5
Atlanta, GA 30307
404-688-1376

National Drug Abuse Hotline
800-662-4357

National Herpes Hotline
919-361-8488

National Institute of Drug Abuse Help-Line
800-662-HELP

National Runaway Switchboard
800-621-4000

National Runaway Switchboard for the Hearing
    Impaired
800-621-0394

National Youth Crisis Hotline
800-442-HOPE

Operation Lookout
    (National Center for Missing Youth)
800-782-SEEK

Parents against Teen Suicide
(teen education and crisis line)
800-367-7287

Parental Stress Services
600 South Federal Street
Suite 205
Chicago, IL 60605
(Twenty-four-hour hotline includes counseling,
    support, problem solving, and referrals)

312-3-PARENT (372-7368)
312-427-1102 (hearing impaired TTY/TDD)

Sexually Transmitted Disease Information Line
800-227-8922

Sexually Transmitted Disease Information and
    Referral
800-653-4325

The Safer Society Program
PO Box 340
Brandon, VT 05733
802-247-3132
(A national project of the New York Council of
    Churches, which maintains a national directory
    of agencies and treatment programs for young
    violent offenders, as well as for abuse victims
    and offenders)

Teen Pregnancy Hotline
800-522-5006

Teens Tap AIDS Hotline
(national aids hotline for teens by teens, sponsored
    by Good Samaritan Project of Kansas City)
800-234-TEEN (234-8336)

Notes

1. Barrie Levy and Patricia Occhiuzzo Giggans, *What Parents Need to Know About Dating Violence* (Seattle: Seal Press, n.d.), 161–62.

2. "Health Care Providers as Protectors," *The Interchange for Mental Health Professionals* (December 1993): 9.

3. *For Shelter and Beyond: Ending Violence against Battered Women and Their Children*, Massachusetts Coalition of Battered Women Service Groups.

4. See, for example, P. A. Gwartney-Gibbs, "Learning Courtship Aggression: The Influence of Parents, Peers, and Personal Experiences," *Family Relations* 36 (1987): 276–82.

5. D. Levinson, *Family Violence in Cross-Cultural Perspective* (Newbury Park, CA: Sage, 1989).

6. M. A. Straus et al., *Behind Closed Doors: Violence in the American Family* (New York: Doubleday, 1980): 121.

7. See Feingold et al, *Psychology*, 2nd ed. (Boston: Houghton Mifflin, 1991), 60.

8. Mary Pipher, *Reviving Ophelia* (New York: Ballantine, 1994).

9. "On the Inside: Children's Beauty Pageants," Discovery Channel, 25 Oct. 1999.

10. *The Developing Child: Understanding Children and Parenting* (New York: Macmillan, 1994).

11. Michele Elliot, "Images of Children in the Media," in atherine Itzin, ed., *Pornography: Women, Violence, and Civil Liberties* (New York: Oxford University Press, 1992.) See also Buchwald et al., *Transforming a Rape Culture* (Minneapolis: Milkweek Editions, 1993).

12. Elizabeth Kaye, "Victims of Fantasy," *The News & Observer,* 9 June 1993.

13. Lawrence A. Garfield et al., *Bureau of Justice Fact Book: Violence by Intimates* (Washington, DC: U.S. Dept. of Justice, March 1998).

14. Per Website of the National Campaign to Prevent Teen Pregnancy (www.teenpregnancy.org.)

15. Patsy Klaus and Michael Rand, *Bureau of Justice Statistics Special Report: Family Violence* (Washington, DC: U.S. Dept. of Justice, 1992).

16. National Coalition Against Domestic Violence, 1992.

17. *Bureau of Justice Statistics: National*

Crime Victimization Survey (Washington, DC: U.S. Dept. of Justice, August 1995).

18. The battering cycle was first described in Lenore Walker, *The Battered Woman* (New York: Harper & Row, 1979).

19. Domestic Abuse Intervention Project, Minnesota Program Development, Inc., 202 East Superior St., Duluth, MN 55802.

20. Ibid.

21. Gwartney-Gibbs, "Learning Courtship Aggression," 276–82.

22. In one study, 25 percent of high school students told no one, only 26 percent told their parents, and 66 percent told their friends: J. Henton et al, "Romance and Violence in Dating Relationships," *Journal of Family Issues* 4 (1993): 467–82.

23. American Psychological Association, *Violence and Youth: Psychology's Response* (Washington, DC: APA, 1993).

24. National Coalition Against Domestic Violence, Action Notes (1989).

25. Ibid.

26. Diana Baumrind, "Early Socialization and Adolescent Competence," in S. E. Dragastin and G. H. Elder, eds., *Adolescence in the Life Cycle* (New York: Wiley, 1985).

27. Gwartney-Gibbs, "Learning Courtship Aggression," 276–82.

28. B. S. Centerwell, "Exposure to Television as a Cause of Violence," in G. Comstock, ed., *Public Communication and Behavior* 2 (San Diego: Academic Press, 1989); also L. D. Eron, "The Development of Aggressive Behavior from the Perspective of a Developing Behaviorism," *American Psychologist* 42 (1987): 435–42.

29. W. L. Josephson, "Television Violence and Children's Aggression: Testing the Priming, Social Script, and Disinhibition Predictions," *Journal of Personality and Social Psychology* 53 (1987): 882– 90.

30. M. Bograd, *Women and Family Therapy* (Rockville, MD: Aspen, 1986); also E. Carmen et al., "Victims of Violence and Psychiatric Illness," *American Journal of Psychiatry* 141 (1994): 378, 383.

31. M. Perog-Good and J. Stets Kealy, *Male Batters and Battering Prevention Programs: A National Survey.*

32. Marie Fortune, *Keeping the Faith: Guidance for Christian Women Facing Abuse* (New York: Harper Collins, 1987), 52.

33. Ibid., 53.